Daintree
...to the Coral Sea

Daintree ...to the Coral Sea

PHOTOGRAPHY BY PETER JARVER
MASTER OF PHOTOGRAPHY, AIPP

TEXT BY ROD RITCHIE

THUNDERHEAD PUBLISHING
CAIRNS - AUSTRALIA

FAR North Queensland is blessed with an unusual variety of environments, which meet to form a conjunction of World Heritage importance. The state's highest mountains snake their way up the east coast of Australia, hugging the coastline with their often mist-shrouded peaks. Precipitous ravines have been carved by fast flowing creeks and rivers, sometimes swollen by immense tropical downpours. The south-east trade winds which prevail here collide with this mountainous barrier to produce substantial clouds, which in turn provide a high annual rainfall, the lifeblood of tropical rainforests.

Evolving millions of years ago, the rainforests of this mountainous area are the oldest continuously surviving forests on earth. Enduring many cycles of Ice Ages and aeons of continental drift, these forests contain the most diverse flora and fauna in Australia.

Adjacent to this spectacular mainland environment is an equally spectacular marine environment, the Great Barrier Reef. Stretching for 2,500 kilometres parallel to the coast in relatively shallow waters, the Reef consists of thousands of individual reefs and hundreds of continental islands, coral cays and atolls. In a few places, this spectacular World Heritage listed reef meets the rainforest-clad mountains of the Wet Tropics, a rare conjunction matched almost nowhere else in the world.

Hundreds of thousands of people visit this area each year. Great catamarans whisk day-trippers by the hundreds to the reef for a day of snorkelling, and eco-tours transport dozens at a time to marvellous rainforests complete with ferns, vines and enormous buttress root trees.

But modern living has become so fast that many of us expect instant gratification and we have forgotten about, or have no time for, seeking out subtleties. The underwater world, with its exotic and colourful environment, can offer an intense and immediate experience.

The rainforests have a more familiar feel but leave us in awe of their profusion of vines, ferns and epiphytes, and the diversity and density of the plants. Our eyes become adapted to the lower levels of light, but what do they really see? What do we notice apart from an imposing forest giant and the overwhelming tangle of green?

We often fail to see past first impressions because we have little time to absorb and learn. Walking is a great way to slow down and appreciate our surroundings. Better still is to find a comfortable, shady spot and observe the lush environment. Look, listen, smell and feel your surroundings. The very essence of nature is in its subtle nuances. The patterns, the shapes, the texture and the colours, all help to define our response.

In a landscape crowded with visual elements, it may be difficult to see the wood for the trees. We need to sit quietly and observe for a while, distilling down the many elements, until we begin to realise what it is that has captured our attention.

Photography gives me a strong reason to immerse myself in a natural environment. To observe, to listen and to feel the spirit of nature is relaxing and fulfilling in itself, but to bring home images which capture the very essence of a place or a moment is truly satisfying. Time and time again I am able to transport myself to a particular place, or remember a magical moment of time when the quality of light transformed the ordinary into the extraordinary.

We have largely ceased our interaction with nature and its spiritual energy. Disconnected from the soul of our existence, we live in a plugged-in, manufactured world. But try immersing yourself in the vibrancy of the forest or the kaleidoscope of colours and shapes that is the domain of the coral reef. Avoid being hurried when you do so and the experience may well convince you of the need for wild and undeveloped places. Rediscover the beauty and tranquillity of nature. Rest your inner spirit and remove yourself from the frantic pace of modern life.

There is no better place to do so than the reefs and rainforests of Far North Queensland.

Peter Janney

CONTENTS

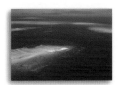

MOUNTAINS OF MIST

THE LANDSCAPE of Far North Queensland is dominated by the rugged coastal ranges which make up the northern part of Australia's major mountain system, the Great Dividing Range. Draped in green, cut by fast flowing streams and often shrouded in mist or cloud, these dramatic mountains remain in the minds of all who fall under their spell. The moist sea air strikes this inland barrier, rises and condenses to form voluminous clouds which provide a high annual rainfall to the surrounding area. This creates a micro-climate for the ancient forests which clothe the mountainsides and provide refuge for many unique animals which have become adapted to this environment. Fog often hugs the treetops. On the high peaks, covered in cloud much of the time, are found the 'cloud forests', their distinctive, sparse flora dependent on aspect, drainage and moisture for their form.

Queensland's two highest mountains, Mt Bartle Frere and Mt Bellenden Ker, both with peaks nearly 1,600 metres above sea-level, are geological wonders with a spiritual past. They also form part of an extensive wilderness national park recently renamed Wooroonooran. Several types of forest exist within the park, depending on the elevation, ranging from dense lowland rainforests to wind-swept, low-lying heath on the areas above 1,500 metres. The tops of the mountains are a complex of peaks and hanging valleys, of bald slopes and huge, lichen-covered boulders.

The geological origins of these mountains can be traced back 300 million years to when underground movement caused pools of molten rock to rise towards the earth's surface, where they slowly cooled to become extensive underground deposits of granite. Sea levels began to fall 100 million years ago; continental uplifting and subsequent erosion of earlier-formed sedimentary rock exposed the granite batholiths to form the basis of the present landform. During the last few million years and as recently as 10,000 years ago, volcanic activity produced extensive lava flows which weathered to become the rich, red basaltic soils of the Atherton Tableland. Another interesing landform, just south of Cairns, is the distinctive Walsh's Pyramid, a conical, volcanic granite intrusion.

Mt Bartle Frere was first climbed in 1886 by the venturesome Christie Palmerston who, following the time-honoured tradition of marking the 'conquered' landscape, carved his name in a tree at the summit. Local Aborigines, while being known to scale the slopes, would never attempt the climb to the tops of these mountains. The reverence in which they held them was tinged with a fear that the great spirit Murgalainya would one day return to its resting place. Aborigines infused the landscape with a mythology that regarded it as a living entity with connections to a Dreamtime from whence all life evolved. When Europeans disturbed this harmony and cleared the lowland and tableland vegetation to make way for settlement and agriculture, the forested mountain-sides were left largely intact. Recently, the mountain forests from Townsville to Cooktown were afforded protection as part of the Wet Tropics World Heritage Area.

A dramatic time to observe the mountains and their surroundings is at sunrise or sunset. Gazing out to sea from a mountain lookout at dawn, it is possible to see a bright yellow glow through a break in the clouds as the sun clears the horizon. Patchy remnants of cloud from an early morning shower hover before being scorched into oblivion by the rising sun. The headland becomes barely visible as the light defines its presence on the silvery film of the calm, morning sea. A glance back to Mt Bellenden Ker reveals the peak, highlighted as the first of the sun's rays strike the mountain tops. In the afternoon, shafts of sunlight filter down to reflect the river and sea. Fleetingly, the silhouetted mountains form a craggy, dark presence before night falls.

Sunrise on the Atherton Tableland is a more tranquil experience. Sheets of filmy, low cloud cover the ground before dissipating with the advance of the new day. Cool nights and milder daytime temperatures give the Tableland a more temperate climate than the humid coast and lowlands. Seen from above, downy, white clouds sink into the landform's undulations. Often when the mist is on the edge of the tableland, it appears to spill down the mountainside, shrouding the ravines in white. In contrast, at sunset the mountain ranges present shaded ridges of varying depth as the evening light melds into the haze of the descending storm clouds.

The riverbed of 'The Boulders', at the base of Bellenden Ker, is strewn with huge, water-worn granite rocks sculpted by the turbulent waters of Babinda Creek. The average of six metres of rainfall which the district receives annually constantly replenishes the waters of the creek. The patterns of light and shade on the rocks, which have been smoothed by the constant grinding of rock sediments, cause visitors to gaze in awe at their unique appearance. It is a place with mythical significance to the local Aboriginal people who claim that, in times long past, the beautiful young Oolana threw herself into the stream after being separated from her lover. Ever since, according to the legend, the waters have lured young men to their deaths.

Away from the wetter areas, open eucalypt woodlands dominate the drier, exposed ridges; the wiry tufts of the slow-growing grasstrees complementing the fine needles of the she-oaks. These forests are found on the western slopes of the mountain ranges where the rainfall is modest compared to the wetter east. The eucalypts, with an understorey of native grasses, have developed as a fire-resistant alternative to the moist forests, and often act as a buffer zone to the rainforests. In the gullies, wet sclerophyll forests thrive; the trunks of tall eucalypts shed strips of exfoliating bark, revealing peculiar patterns, rich colours and a variety of textures.

Mountain streams feed the major river systems which wind their way through the canefields of the coastal plains to drain into the Coral Sea. Along the Mulgrave River,

in the Goldsborough Valley, the matted root systems of the tenacious water gums maintain their grip despite regular deluges and ever-changing river heights. The waterways support a variety of plant life which thrives in the constant dampness. Pools, ringed with moss-clad rocks and hanging ferns, are formed and fed by waterfalls such as the spectacular Josephine Falls in Woonoorooran National Park. Here groves of leaning River Cherries line the river banks.

Mountain streams are sometimes dammed as catchments to supply water for the towns and cities. From the panoramic vista of Lamb's Head it is possible to see the waters of Lake Morris, the lifeblood of Cairns. Here stunted, windswept vegetation fills the crevices of spectacular rocky outcrops atop sheer rockfaces which descend to the forests below. Further back in the mountains at Tully Falls, the river system has been harnessed to provide hydro-electricity and the visitor is restricted to cliff-edge lookouts with rugged mountain views. Here you can only visualise mute torrents tumbling into imaginary pools. However, when rain-bearing cyclones dump their load, the volume of water becomes too great and escapes man's grasp.

During the wet season, the swollen waterways swiftly find their way down to the lowlands via a series of granite outcrops which become raging waterfalls. Standing at a vantage point overlooking the largest of these, the Barron Falls, is an overwhelming experience. Visitors stare mesmerised, as the foaming cataract tumbles over the edge, sending a fine spray upwards to mingle with wisps of overhanging mist. Further down, the feathery rush of water surges around the gnarled rocks on its way to the valley several hundred metres below. Bright green sedges and ferns cling to the rock sides, sustained by the misty vapours, as shafts of light filter down to highlight the scant vegetation of the hillside.

These fast flowing streams and waterfalls, deep gorges and forested mountains have long attracted visitors to Far North Queensland. At the turn of the last century, one writer foresaw the region's great recreation potential, observing that it would be a *'future paradise of the artist and the lovers of the beautiful, the scenery-hunting tourists of years to come'* when the mountains became familiar to *'amateur explorers'*. These words were prophetic. The same observer despaired the consequences of this attention, since the day-trippers then had a tendency to leave their *'sardine tins… sandwich wrappers, and infernal rum bottles'* at the sites. Today, more enlightened visitors realise that their favourite places are in danger of being 'loved to death' and that the future of these vital ecosystems lies in our hands.

Morning light reveals Cairns' mountainous backdrop, including the Whitfield Range, Walsh's Pyramid and Mount Bellenden Ker.

The last glow of sunset shows the mountainous barrier which confines Cairns to the narrow coastal strip adjoining Trinity Inlet.

Rainforest-clad ridges stretch well beyond the Lamb Range in this 70 kilometre view to Mount Bartle Frere.

Shafts of sunlight penetrate a gap in the clouds over Mount Bellenden Ker, highlighting numerous ridges.

Glimpsed through a break in the early morning cloud, the rising sun illuminates the sweep of Cape Grafton.

Layers of cloud cloak the Barron Valley while only loftier hills bask in the morning sun.

The Atherton Tableland cradles pockets of morning fog as the Great Dividing Range looms in the distance.

Morning fog from the Atherton Tableland cascades down the slopes of the Macalister Range.

The breathtaking view from Lamb's Head encompasses Lake Morris, Cairns city and the Coral Sea beyond.

The imposing monolith of Kahlpahlim overlooks the Atherton Tableland towards Mareeba.

The mighty Barron Falls thunders over a 200 metre drop to the valley below.

Drenching spray buffets a few hardy plants at the base of Barron Falls, survivors of raging wet season torrents.

An island of rock, resembling a man's head, defies the plunging flood waters of the Barron River.

The morning sun highlights a tree clinging precariously to the side of Barron Gorge, as spray from the falls drifts by.

Crystal clear water from Mount Bartle Frere tumbles down Josephine Falls.

A sturdy root system anchors these trees as they lean defiantly over Josephine Creek.

These tumbled granite rocks, known as The Boulders, are continuously washed by the clear mountain waters of Babinda Creek, runoff from Mount Bartle Frere.

Fresh mountain water slides over polished granite slabs at The Boulders.

Water trickles down the smooth surface of a large granite boulder.

Water-sculptured shapes at The Boulders belie the strength and durability of granite.

Mist obscures the steep sides of Tully Gorge.

Grasstrees cling tenaciously to the windswept summit of a coastal mountain as mist softens the morning light.

Rising over 1,100 metres, Australia's largest island national park, Hinchinbrook Island, is silhouetted in this dawn view from Mission Beach.

Rays of sunlight pierce the morning sky, highlighting the canefields of Cairns and Cape Grafton beyond.

FORESTS OF RAIN

THE RUGGED Great Dividing Range, inland from the coast of eastern Australia, forms a physical barrier between the dry plains in the west and the lush coastal river valleys. This forested, mountainous expanse supports a variety of rainforests which occur in patches from Tasmania to Cape York Peninsula. They occupy the wetter, sheltered, often volcanic soils of the hills and valleys in this mountain system, and the edges of the coastal rivers and their tributaries linking the mountains to the sea. Significantly, they vary in structure from temperate in the south through sub-tropical in the mid-latitudes, to the complex tropical forests of North Queensland. Nowhere are these ancient, wet forests more profuse and varied than in the far north where they have earned the title 'Wet Tropics'.

Rainforests evolved millions of years ago when the continental land mass of present-day Australia was a part of the super-continent, Gondwana. Over one hundred million years ago almost the entire country was covered in these forests. However, over the years, climatic variation and continental movement altered the patterns of vegetation, and rainforests have advanced and receded accordingly. Eucalypts and wattles emerged as adapters to a drying climate and the resulting increased incidence of fire. In the last 40,000 years, Aboriginal habitation became a further determining factor with the introduction of deliberate burning. Eventually, rainforest remnants remained in favourable sites and the fire-tolerant sclerophyll vegetation became predominant elsewhere.

For thousands of years groups of Aboriginal people lived within the Wet Tropics, sustaining a culture that was unparalleled in Australia. Their ability to process potentially poisonous plants enabled them to survive times of food shortages. Pathways through the rainforests were the routes of travel and trade that formed the basis of their social system. The material culture of the people was unique; women made elaborate string bags and men wove distinctive baskets braided from lawyer cane. Shields were manufactured from the buttresses of trees and decorated in bold geometric designs. Many sites of Aboriginal significance are remembered to this day and the rich tapestry of mythology which infuses the Wet Tropics adds a special dimension to the region.

Tropical rainforests are home to the most diverse flora and fauna in Australia; many of the plants and animals are unique and some are rare or threatened. The birdlife of the rainforests is easily seen and heard on even the shortest walk, although the largest of Australia's birds, the rare, flightless Cassowary, may be harder to find. The Wet Tropics is also home to unique marsupials which are relics of the animal life that inhabited the forests in ages past. Many of the species live only in small, distinct areas and are found nowhere else in the world. Endangered or threatened species include the Brush-tailed Bettong, the Spotted-tailed Quoll, the Mahogany Glider and the northern race of the Yellow-bellied Glider. Several other species of animals have very restricted distribution, including the Atherton Antechinus, Thornton Peak Rat and various frogs and reptiles. Visitors who take time to observe rainforests and their inhabitants cannot help but appreciate their beauty and significance.

The Wet Tropics region, which has been described as *'a living museum of unique flora and fauna'* and *'one of the most significant regional ecosystems in the world'*, contains 13 of the world's 19 primitive flowering plant families, the angiosperms. As living fossils they hold the clue to the evolution of the flowering plants. Botanists studying the rainforests here have suggested that many of the plants have endured continuously since early times and are virtual clones of plants found in Gondwanan forests. This makes the experience of walking in the half-light of the luxuriant, ancient rainforest an awe-inspiring experience.

This feeling of being in a timeless environment is particularly evident in the coastal lowland rainforests where hundreds of species of trees compete with each other, and plants grow on plants in search of the scarcest commodity of all - light. The diversity of plant life is astonishing. As you tread your way, you can observe the verdant mass of diverse vegetation with epiphytes, mosses and climbers all struggling upwards. Giant, often buttressed, trees have their head foliage way out of sight, with only fallen leaves or fruit or a knowledge of bark types giving a clue to their identity. On the decaying forest floor, a variety of mosses, lichens and fungi attack and live on a mass of rotting debris which is being rapidly absorbed back into its surroundings.

On the uplands of Daintree National Park, the huge forest sentinels rise through the mist, dwarfing their surroundings and especially humans who appear as only a minor intrusion in this riot of growth. Like the majestic eucalypts in the wet sclerophyll forests, these forest giants have survived the days of timber-cutting, when many tree species attained the status of gold. Rainforests are often called vine forests because of the ropy, often twisted lianes which stretch from the forest floor to the canopy. While the epiphytes cling to the trees, the spreading tentacles of plant-life reach out for a hold. All around, a multitude of vines, including the ubiquitous barbed 'wait-a-while', clinging epiphytes and countless varieties of plants, compete for attention.

A myriad of small ferns and a variety of flowering plants add to the botanical profusion. Trees such as the Bumpy Satinash, which have flowers and fruit emerging directly from the trunk, surprise the visitor. This growth form, known as 'cauliflory', has evolved to make use of the animal highways so as to maximise chances for pollination and seed dispersal. At Cape Tribulation the leaves of the distinctive fan palms, Licuala ramsayii, present a bold outline. Often growing at their bases, the seemingly infinite wait-a-while, as its name implies, makes passage in the forest a chore.

The Curtain Fig, on the Atherton Tableland, with its massive veils of roots hanging down from a diagonal trunk, demonstrates the other plant necessity - nourishment from the moist soil. Another tableland attraction, the majestic Cathedral Fig, having long strangled its host tree, is a mass of matted, angled, fused roots as it stands cathedral-like to dominate its surroundings. Nowhere is the 'gothic' feel of the rainforest more evident than when you gaze up at this tree.

The cooler forests of the tablelands favour the tree ferns. Cyanthii Cooperii grows in the light of a canopy gap or perhaps a tree fall, its feathery crown filtering the light, its silhouette a delicate lace against the sky. Stinging trees also thrive in a forest disturbance and are more likely encountered on a forest walking trail than deep in the forest. Amongst the moss-covered granite boulders of an upland stream bed, the 'coral' fern thrives; here the rocks along the banks are often mottled with lichens.

Winding their way, the watercourses ebb and flow with the varying precipitation feeding the larger streams and rivers. Many can become torrents after the seasonal rains. Along the banks the twisted roots of the River Cherry have a tenuous hold. Occasionally an overhanging branch, laden with dripping leaves, will become sufficiently heavy to topple a tree, or a savage flood will dislodge the matted root system which was apparently well-anchored in the watercourse. When the deluge subsides and the waterway returns to a slow trickle, the fallen tree struggles to regain its vertical stance, often taking a curious, contorted form.

At the turn of the last century, when logging for the valuable species diminished, the mountain forests became the favoured visiting places. The Barron Falls, at Kuranda, became a major attraction, particularly after the railway had been opened in 1893. One of the first people to make the journey up the mountain by rail, Ellis Rowan, observed that the deep precipices were countered by towering masses of *'wild tropical vegetation, sometimes palms, vines, bananas, or fairy draperies of hanging ferns; sometimes clusters of orchids, with scarlet flametrees here and there, giving light and brilliant colour to the dense masses of vivid greens, which range from the palest apple and russet to the deepest olive'*.[1]

Today, the experience of travelling on the Kuranda train, as it winds its way up the mountainside to the 'village in the rainforest', is similar. Alternatively, when travelling above the rainforest on the aerial gondola, the Skyrail, it is possible to experience a unique perspective that was previously the domain of birds and helicopter passengers.

Compared to the more familiar, drier, open eucalypt forests, the rainforests in Australia have always appeared exotic and in years gone by were valued for little more than their potential to supply timber or for the land on which they stood. However, most people now appreciate and enjoy them, as well as being educated as to their global importance at a time when, in some countries, their very existence is under threat. Fortunately, the rainforests of North Queensland were preserved after a long campaign by conservationists. Now with recent World Heritage listing and security guaranteed by the Wet Tropics Management Authority they will be there for the protection of the plants and animals and for future generations of visitors to enjoy.

Tall Syzygium trees rise majestically into the mist-shrouded cathedral rainforest in Daintree National Park.

Delicate palms, ferns and lilies compete for space and light in a complex upland rainforest environment.

In a small clearing of the Lamb Range, rocks and tree trunks play host to a profusion of epiphytes, climbers and moss.

Powerful limbs of the awesome Cathedral Fig appear to push back the surrounding canopy to gain more space for this rainforest giant of the Atherton Tableland.

Rosegum trunks follow invisible lines to reach the forest canopy on a drier westerly slope of the Lamb Range.

The feathery fronds of a mountain treefern colony spread gracefully in a sheltered rainforest pocket of the Macalister Range.

Lush rainforest surrounds the picturesque Nandroya Falls in Wooroonooran National Park.

Clear cool water from Mossman Gorge has carved a boulder-strewn path through the Daintree rainforest.

Contorted by wet season flows, this large fig is determined to maintain its stance despite the sandy creek.

Anchored by powerful roots these water gums stand defiantly along the banks of the Mulgrave River.

A cluster of vines hang from high in the canopy.

Cauliflorous pattern on a Bumpy Satinash trunk.

The lichen-patched trunk of a Kauri tree.

Creeping up the buttressed trunk of a Spurwood tree.

Aerial roots of the Curtain Fig plunge to the floor in a remnant patch of rainforest on the Atherton Tableland.

Long, sinewy fingers of a buttressed-root fig stretch out across the rainforest floor.

A hollowed grasstree trunk makes an excellent refuge for the Red-cheeked Dunnart.

Emerging for the night's activity, a Coppery Brushtailed Possum leaves the safety of its hollow trunk.

With its tail wrapped tightly, a young Striped Possum clings to its mother for the evening's food search.

The rare and magnificent white Lemuroid Possum.

A Ring-tailed Possum scouring the canopy for insects and nectar.

Confined to Wet Tropics rainforest, this spectacular and primeval looking Boyd's Forest Dragon displays its throat pouch.

The Cassowary is the largest rainforest inhabitant.

The gaudy Purple Crowned Pigeon is a major disperser of smaller rainforest seeds.

Moss covered rocks host delicate ferns along a cool mountain stream bordered by rainforest.

Rainforest overhangs a small tributary of Mossman River, which is littered with granite rocks worn smooth by the water.

Delicate fronds of the tree fern feather the breezes on a rainforest slope near Mount Alexandra.

The fronds of the unusual fan palm, Licuala Ramsayi, have a stunning circular shape.

An old vine trunk loops aimlessly across some boulders as it continues its journey through the rainforest.

The apparent confusion of this old vine tells many stories about the trees that once occupied this patch of rainforest.

Thick lengths of vine traverse the rocky creek which has forged a path between the rainforest trees.

Numerous aerial roots support the enormous branches of a Banyan-like fig on the shore of Lake Barrine.

OUT BACK
OF THE TABLELAND

THE OUTBACK evokes classic images that depict the Australian ethos. The North Queensland Outback or Gulf Savannah, that expanse of country west of the Great Dividing Range, is even now a frontier for European settlement. It is also that huge part of the state which is sparsely populated and rarely visited by people who cling to the comforts of coastal cities. While Aboriginal communities are reclaiming their identity and their homelands, there is a yawning gap between the city dwellers' perceptions of these wide open spaces and the reality of life 'back of beyond'.

Immense cloudless skies remain unchanged from day to day, with a monotony born of apparent unchanging seasons. This sameness is deceptive however, as there are two distinct seasons during which the landscape alters dramatically. Plants and animals have evolved to make the most of this change. Vegetation may be sparse and resistant to the extremes of weather, but the muted greens of the trees and shrubs and the straw yellow of the grasses complement the dominant colours of this northern outback - the reds and browns of the earth and the deep-blue skies.

The arrival of the Wet season is heralded by gathering storm clouds which build on the horizon and eventually cast a dark shadow over all. The flooding rains transform the landscape into one of bounty unimaginable when compared to countryside in dry times. This abundance can be seen around the billabongs which teem with colourful flowering plants and swarm with insect life. Fish breed in the rivers and lagoons. The migratory birds, which are annually attracted to nest and feed their young on nature's surplus, are a dramatic sight as they arrive to take advantage of this transitory feast.

At the other extreme, in the Dry season, animals keep within range of the waterholes which shrink down to muddy puddles. The Outback appears comatose when daytime temperatures range in the high thirties for weeks at a time. Even the hardiest of plants must rely on their extensive root systems to survive. In the middle of the day the sun beats down and animal life seeks the shade or the relative cool of deep burrows. In the evenings and at night the landscape comes to life with the collective activity of the nocturnal marsupials and reptiles which emerge to feed.

Millions of stars fill the night sky and glow with a clarity that those living with the glare of city lights have never experienced. Those fortunate enough to have slept under this astronomical excess experience a tranquillity undreamed of. Dry electrical storms sweep through on occasions and illuminate the sky with brilliant flashes that silhouette the sparse vegetation and ancient landforms. When rain finally falls, the smell of wet soil and plants gives the impression of instant fecundity, although this can be short-lived as moisture from light showers is quickly dissipated by the morning sun.

Although the Outback experience can be harsh, the rewards for perseverance are many. Travellers must learn the rhythms of this dry, dusty land to get the most out of a visit, and should be prepared to adapt. Rough roads and lack of amenities at overnight stays are only two inconveniences to be faced. If having to illuminate your way by torch to the outside 'thunder-box', with its threat of redbacks under the seat, bothers you, then think carefully before embarking on your journey.

Beef production is still the economic mainstay for the majority of those who make the outback their home, but the days when large teams of stockmen on horseback were required for the annual cattle muster are largely over - now helicopter cowboys swing into action at round-up time. However, it is still possible to come across a herd of cattle being guided down a remote stock route by hardy, mounted stockmen with faithful dogs at their sides.

A variety of minerals are excavated by a new breed of outback workers who drive the heavy machinery used in open-cut mines. While mining is presently a boom industry, it has long ebbed and flowed with the prices and availability of resources. The small towns that lived and died with the passing of the local mine are being given a new lease on life as new techniques allow for the re-opening of some mines. Many others are being rejuvenated as destinations for outback travellers.

Chillagoe, located to the north-west of the Atherton Tableland, is one of these. This old copper mining town is known as the gateway to the outback and the location of 'coral reefs' of ages past. The distinctive inland limestone bluffs are a reminder that 600 million years ago this area was a coastal region. Planktonic organisms, similar to those found in the Great Barrier Reef waters, dropped skeletons of calcium carbonate over millions of years, forming a thick layer of sediment which eventually was compressed to form limestone. Finally, after major geological upheavals, the shoreline reached its present location.

At Undara, extensive lava tubes remain from a time when volcanic activity dominated the surrounding landscape. The tubes, the largest known to exist, were formed when massive lava streams, moulded by stream beds, cooled quickly on the outside as the inside lava kept moving. The resulting hollow tube, with its solidified outer basaltic crust, can today be entered through fallen roof sections. Inside are unique plants which have adapted to their special surroundings, and hundreds of thousands of bats who have a sound and smell all their own. The primitive rainforest surrounding the tubes is a dense, dark green vine thicket that contrasts with the drier eucalypt-dominated surroundings.

The monumental Magnetic Termite mounds at Lakefield National Park, named for their north-south alignment, are homes to colonies of Amitermes laurensis. The mounds of earth are temperature-controlled since the broad surfaces face the morning and late afternoon sun, while at midday they receive the least heat. Inside, termites store grass and other plant material high in the mound where it is out of reach of the floods which can inundate the plains. A complex system of interconnecting cells houses the queen, who lays the eggs, and the king who mates with her. There are also places for a worker caste for building, a soldier caste for defence and a reproductive caste whose members fly away to start new colonies.

The small town of Laura, with its wide, dusty main street, was once the busy railhead for the Palmer River goldfields. Today, visitors come to see the district's cultural treasures - the Aboriginal rock art galleries within sandstone shelters, some dating back 15,000 years. Depictions of the Quinkans, the Dreamtime spirits of good and evil who roamed the bush, are the work of the Guguyalangi people. So long has been their association with the land, that their ancient renderings of sea creatures is a confirmation of modern geological theories which infer that the coastline was once inland from its present location. Some of the last pictures completed show mounted horsemen; the portent of things to come.

Fire is a predominant force in the Outback. Conflagrations, both deliberate and accidental, sweep through the bush regularly. It is not uncommon to come across a burning landscape, shafts of sunlight filtering through the dense smoke hanging pall-like over the blackened forest. The vegetation, long evolved to handle natural regimes of fire, is genetically programmed to cope and before long new shoots signal life returning to normal. Animals however, must migrate to unburnt feeding grounds or starve.

At an elevation of over 700 metres, the Atherton Tableland has a moist climate several degrees cooler than the coast. Long cleared of its vast rainforest, the Tableland is a prosperous farming district. Dairy cattle graze on lush pastures growing on rich red basaltic soils. Tobacco growing is being replaced by tropical fruit trees, macadamias, avocados and vegetables. The water required for these crops is pumped from the man-made Lake Tinaroo which has a capacity two-thirds the size of Sydney Harbour. The grey-white tree trunks standing within the dam are an unsightly reminder of the former forest.

Even in this verdant landscape contrasts are evident. Around the farm houses, introduced trees such as the Jacaranda, planted to remind the settlers of home, can be seen flowering. The obvious bright green of the tea bushes stands out against the sombre, dark green of the small remnants of rainforest which patch the countryside. As well, extraordinary natural features, relics from the Tableland's volcanic past, include a series of old explosion cones named the Seven Sisters, the crater lakes of Eacham and Barrine and the volcanic pipe at Mt Hypipamee.

Returning to the coastal hinterland, the antithesis of the Outback, the familiar scenery of ever-present canefields and charming small coastal towns, are seen through new eyes. Soon, the Outback becomes a distant memory. But the images of the dry, rugged inland remain in the consciousness; a permanent legacy of an unforgettable experience.

A prominent limestone outcrop protrudes from the drier and less elevated surrounds of Chillagoe.

Vast numbers of termite mounds dominate this open black soil plain in the Gulf Savannah country.

Purple seed cones of the Lotus Lily crowd together on the edge of Red Lily Lagoon during the late Dry season.

Majestic termite mounds, towering up to two metres in height, are scattered across a treeless plain in Lakefield National Park.

Dry season grasses glow warmly as the morning light streams across a hillside near Laura.

A drier slope of the Lamb Range is dominated by Eucalypts interspersed with grasstrees.

The dry eucalypt country west of the Tableland is subject to fire as part of its natural ecology.

Streams of sunlight burst through the dense smoke of a slow-burning fire on a western slope of the Lamb Range.

Late afternoon sunlight streams through the collapsed roof of one of Undara's numerous lava tubes.

A guardian figure, overlain with a crocodile, peers down from the sandstone roof of Cockatoo shelter, Jowalbinna, part of the Quinkan rock-art reserve near Laura.

The Anglican Church and old bell tower service the vast savannah plains around Georgetown in the Gulf country.

This remarkable building continues to defy gravity as it leans towards the Einasleigh Hotel.

Rows of tea bushes sweep down a hillside in the cool elevated country around Topaz.

During their profuse annual flowering, Jacaranda trees carpet the ground with a riot of colour.

An early morning mist cools the scenery at Lake Tinaroo.

The gentle undulating farmland of the Atherton Tableland spreads out before Mount Bartle Frere, Queensland's highest mountain.

Water cascades down the smooth granite face of a waterfall at Davies Creek.

Crystal clear water rushes over polished granite on its way down Emerald Creek on the Atherton Tableland.

Storm clouds build over the Great Dividing Range.

A spectacular thundercloud dumps heavy rain onto the Atherton Tableland.

In this sunrise view over the Atherton Tableland, morning mist highlights numerous ridges and peaks, extending all the way to the North Barnard Islands.

Many mountain ridges are apparent in this sunset view over the Tableland towards the Great Dividing Range.

COASTLINE OF CORAL

COASTAL towns and cities have always been regarded as home by the majority of Australians. Yet the very length of the coastline of this massive island continent has ensured that most of the coast has remained in its natural state, particularly in Far North Queensland. Beach after white beach, interrupted only by rocky headlands and river estuaries, front a turquoise ocean fringed with pale, lace-like reefs. Aboriginal people have fished and collected shell food along the coast for thousands of years, even before the present reefs were formed. Numerous middens and archaeological sites found along the foreshore are testament to their seaside feasts.

The far northern tribes built canoes, some with outriggers, which were capable of being paddled to nearby reefs and offshore islands for fishing and hunting expeditions. European maritime explorers also traversed the waters, their wrecked ships evidence of the perilous nature of the currents and the fierce storms which may sweep in during the cyclone season. But the efforts of humankind hardly register in the time-frame of reef life.

At Cedar Bay, Cape Tribulation and Mission Beach are found the conjunction of two superlative natural systems; unique ecotones where the rainforest meets the fringing reef.

Here, the most complex botanical system on land meets the most diverse aquatic habitat. Although many of the rainforests have been relatively accessible to visitors, only recently has examination of the undersea world been possible without scuba training, expensive equipment and boat hire. Fast catamarans now whisk thousands of travellers a week from Port Douglas and Cairns to the Great Barrier Reef, one of Australia's most visited natural travel destinations. Here they marvel at reefs of luxuriant coral growths and abundant marine life, arguably one of nature's most remarkable accomplishments.

The Great Barrier Reef, stretching from the Torres Strait almost to the Tropic of Capricorn, is a seemingly endless chain of nearly three thousand individual reefs and hundreds of continental islands, coral cays and atolls. Growing in relatively shallow waters, the reef is around 2,500 km long and up to 300 km wide. Often described as the world's largest living structure, the reef should not be regarded as a single entity; rather it is a constantly changing conglomerate of individual reefs and islands continually affected by the elements.

The origin of these reefs goes back millions of years. Changing sea levels alternately flooded and exposed the coastal reefs many times, the corals dying as the sea became either too deep or too shallow, leaving the reefs high and dry. After the end of the last ice age, the ice caps melted to such an extent that the sea reclaimed the coastal lowlands and corals grew once again on the eroded reef platforms of past ages. Thus, the core of a typical coral reef is in fact coral skeletons cemented by coraline algae into coral 'rock'. On this solid base the living coral polyps manufacture exquisite structures which become home to a myriad of colourful fishes, starfishes, worms and molluscs. Rare and endangered whales, turtles and dugongs breed inside this protective barrier.

Although the best photographers portray the reef and its inhabitants with skill and perception, and statistics and superlatives are employed to present its magnitude and beauty, it is only by experiencing the reef and its marine life first-hand that a real understanding of its complexity and immensity can be gained. Nothing prepares you for the profusion of life encountered on a dive in the warm, protected waters around the reefs. The aquatic environment is as finely balanced and diverse as any terrestrial environment and includes hundreds of types of hard and soft corals, thousands of different molluscs, sponges, worms, crustaceans, echinoderms, and more than a thousand different species of fish, all part of a complex food chain. Free-floating plankton, a myriad of microscopic plants and animals, are devoured by small fish and reef invertebrates. These are in turn eaten by larger carnivores such as Coral Trout and Spanish Mackerel, who find themselves a target for larger predators, not the least of which is man.

Bony bodies, poisonous glands and protective colouration are some of the means of defence against the larger carnivores. Also common are symbiotic relationships developed to provide shelter: small fish survive among poisonous tentacles of anemones and jellyfish; fish and crustaceans live among the branches of spiky staghorn coral; and sharks provide safety for the small pilot fish which attach by suction to their underbellies.

Reef fish and invertebrates have adapted to make the most of their hostile environment. For instance, the Parrotfish use their beak-like teeth to scrape algal food from the reef substrate; the red and gold Goatfish have a beard of two bristles which act as sensory organs; the elongated snout of the Beaked coral fish has evolved to probe deep into coral crevices for food. Under coral overhangs, often found on the side of bommies, live brightly coloured sponges, ascidians, gorgonians and soft corals, and many of the smaller fish seeking shelter from larger predators. Burrowed into the top of a coral bommie the unique feather-duster worm unfurls its brilliantly coloured tentacles to trap unwary prey.

Each year the reef hosts a sensational display of coral spawning, which begins just after the full moon in late spring or early summer. In the preceding months the sex organs of coral polyps, often containing both male and female gonads, ready themselves, and in the warming spring waters the sex cells begin to develop. When conditions are optimal, the eggs and sperm are simultaneously released and the waters become a coloured mass of reproductive cells. This behaviour ensures a high rate of fertilisation for the stationary coral polyp.

The continental islands and coral cays provide destinations in which the experience of snorkelling the reef and viewing the land-based plants and animals can be combined. Low Isles, located off Port Douglas and aptly named by James Cook in 1770, is barely visible from any distance. The two cay islets, one supporting mangroves, are part of an ever-changing reef structure formed by the rubble of dead coral and other sediments, and provide a rich breeding ground for marine and birdlife. Tiny Michaelmas Cay, on the outer Great Barrier Reef off Cairns, appears to float on the translucent Coral Sea. Beneath these blue-green waters, colourful fish dart in and out among the branching corals. Each year many species of seabirds, including Sooty terns, Reef herons, gulls, Shearwaters, boobies, gannets and Frigate birds, come to the cay to nest. This popular coral-viewing and bird-watching destination has diving pontoons and fenced-off nesting areas – an attempt to limit the impacts of mass tourism.

Legislation protecting the reef's inhabitants has been introduced to ensure that conservation strategies are implemented as an important step towards ecological sustainability. In 1981 the Great Barrier Reef region achieved the ultimate protection of being inscribed on the World Heritage List.

Fringed by reef, Snapper Island, just off Cape Kimberley at the mouth of the Daintree River, is a continental island – one which derived from the mainland after the changing sea levels of the last ice age. Another such continental remnant, Dunk Island, located off the coast at Mission Beach, supports a contrasting array of tropical flora and fauna, including rainforests and their inhabitants. Walking trails allow exploration of the diverse terrain, from its sandy beaches to its forested hills and valleys. The summit of Mt Kootaloo, overlooking the Family Islands and distant reefs, is a great place to contemplate the formation of this unique eco-system.

The Far North Queensland beaches are often battered by wind-chopped seas whipped up by tropical cyclones, which leave the shores littered with coral remains. Barnacle-encrusted rocky prominences abut the headlands, their sculptured forms worn by the sea. At Coopers Creek, in Cape Tribulation National Park, the strand communities of Red mangroves grow near the sea in areas protected from high swells, with angled roots perched in the rich silt. At the Hull River estuary can be found Coastal pandanus with their distinctive prop roots. Away from the shore, swamp forests of paperbarks, with a ground cover of water ferns, survive the seasonal inundations and prevailing winds.

A cloudless sunrise in the tropics is often accompanied by a fleeting luminescent half-light as the sun returns to the horizon. A day spent on a tropical beach in the shade of weeping she-oaks is an incomparable experience. At sunset, palms are silhouetted against the orange sky and a calm evening sea laps the shore with a rhythm dictated by the tide. The fast-fading sunlight highlights the clouds. Looking out to sea it is hard to imagine that the reef in all its immensity and complexity even exists.

Mangroves colonize Woody Island and a lighthouse marks the position of Low Island, together known as the Low Isles.

Once part of the mainland, Dunk Island is only a short sail from Mission Beach.

Sitting astride a narrow spit of land, Port Douglas follows the sweep of Four Mile Beach.

Shallow water highlights the reef surrounding Green Island, with Fitzroy Island and the mainland mountains visible in the distance.

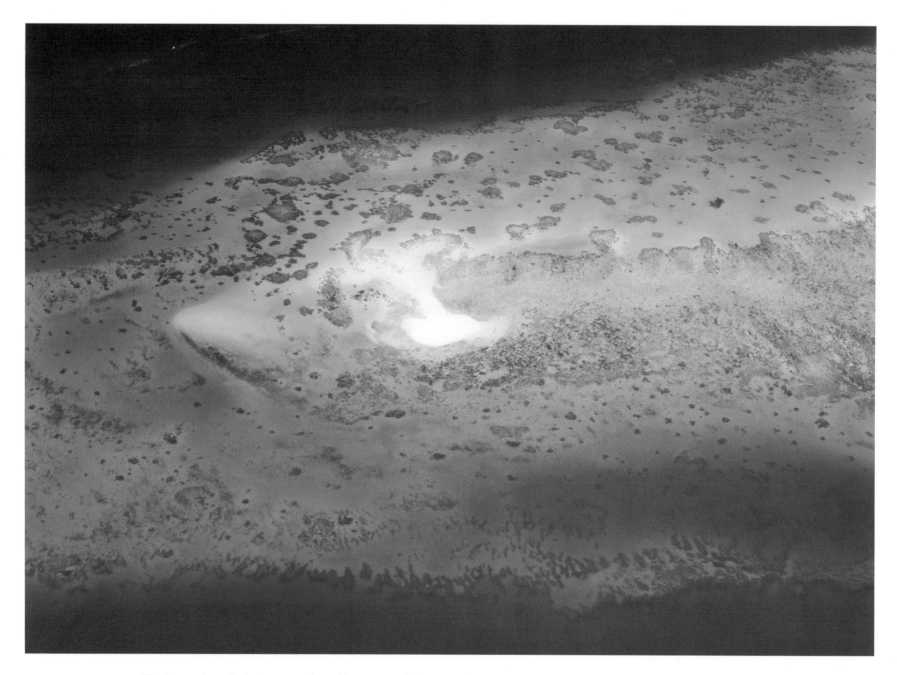

The interaction of wind, wave and coral have created the beautiful patterns of Undine Reef and produced a tiny sand cay.

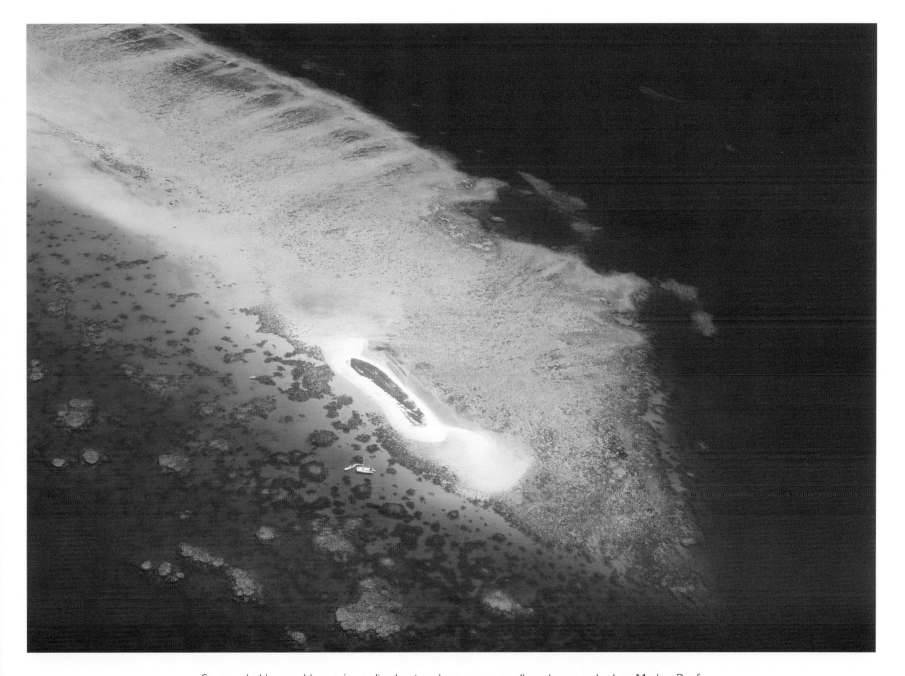

Surrounded by coral bommies, a dive boat anchors near a small sand cay perched on Mackay Reef.

Divers share the reef with numerous fish as the dive ship is silhouetted against the midday sun.

A school of Goldman's Sweetlips patrols the waters of the Cod Hole near Cooktown.

A swirl of Gold-striped Goatfish, schooling at the Temple of Doom bommie.

Purple Anthias streak past a diver inspecting soft corals at the Pixies Pinnacle.

A Coral Rock-Cod seeks refuge among soft corals in a sheltered alcove.

With strong teeth for hunting molluscs and crustaceans, a Harlequin Tuskfish patrols its territory.

An excellent example of a commensal relationship, a jellyfish provides safe refuge for tiny fish which help it to stay clean.

With tentacles extended, a colony of Yellow Daisy Coral feeds at night.

The rocky outcrop at Taylor Point affords an excellent view south to Yorkey's Knob and Cape Grafton beyond.

Cape Kimberley casts a long shadow as the morning sun reddens Hall's Point at the mouth of the Daintree River.

The fiery colour of dawn delineates Buchan Point and Double Island against the distant backdrop of Mount Yarrabah.

Two fishermen try their luck as the intensifying glow heralds the approach of sunrise.

Sunset over the Coral Sea outlines Snapper Island, just off the coast of Cape Kimberley.

Coquette Point at the mouth of the Johnstone River, silhouetted against the hills surrounding Innisfail.

A small colony of pandanus clings to the high-water line of Double Island.

Dune grasses creep out of the forest onto the sand near Cape Tribulation.

Delicate stilt roots support the spindly trunks of a pandanus colony growing along the high-water line of South Mission Beach.

Paperbark trees stand amidst a flourish of ferns only metres from the waves of Lugger Bay.

Rainforest spills down from Mount Neville to the beach, where sturdy mangroves keep a tenacious hold in white sand.

Solitary mangroves defy time and tide in their precarious position at Donovan Point.

Haycock and Double Island lay close off-shore to Buchan Point, Palm Cove.

Fresh south-east trade winds push numerous white-capped waves onto the rocks at Archer Point near Cooktown.

As the lighthouse beam sweeps the evening waters, sunset colours the sky over the Low Isles.

A full moon rises near Green Island, the small coral cay a mere dot in the vast Coral Sea.

TECHNICAL DATA

Cover	Plaubel 69W, Schneider 47mm f 5.6
P.8	Davies 6x9cm, Nikkor 360mm ED f 8, polarizer
P.9	Davies 6x9cm, Schneider 150mm f 5.6
P.10	Davies 6x9cm, Nikkor 360mm ED f 8
P.11	Horseman FA 4x5, Schneider 150mm f 5.6
P.12	Rollei 6006 6x6cm, Rolleigon 50mm f 4
P.13	Davies 6x9cm, Schneider 150mm f 5.6
P.14	Davies 6x9cm, Schneider 150mm f 5.6
P.15	Davies 6x9cm, Schneider 150mm f 5.6
P.16	Davies 6x9cm, Schneider 65mm f 5.6, polarizer
P.17	Davies 6x9cm, Schneider 65mm f 5.6, polarizer
P.18	Horseman FA 4x5, Schneider 90mm f 8
P.19	Davies 6x9cm, Schneider 150mm f 5.6, polarizer
P.20	Davies 6x9cm, Nikkor 360mm ED f 8, polarizer
P.21	Horseman FA 4x5, Nikkor 360mm ED f 8, polarizer
P.22	Davies 6x9cm, Schneider 65mm f 5.6, polarizer
P.23	Davies 6x9cm, Schneider 65mm f 5.6, polarizer
P.24	Horseman FA 4x5, Schneider 150mm f 5.6, polarizer
P.25	Horseman FA 4x5, Schneider 90mm f 8, polarizer
P.26	Horseman FA 4x5, Schneider 90mm f 8, polarizer
P.27	Davies 6x9cm, Schneider 65mm f 5.6
P.28	Davies 6x9cm, Schneider 150mm f 5.6
P.29	Davies 6x9cm, Schneider 65mm f 5.6, polarizer
P.30	Davies 6x9cm, Nikkor 360mm ED f 8
P.31	Davies 6x9cm, Schneider 150mm f 5.6
P.34	Plaubel 69W, Schneider 47mm f 5.6, polarizer
P.35	Plaubel 69W, Schneider 47mm f 5.6, polarizer
P.36	Davies 6x9cm, Schneider 65mm f 5.6, polarizer
P.37	Plaubel 69W, Schneider 47mm f 5.6, polarizer
P.38	Davies 6x9cm, Nikkor 360mm ED f 8, polarizer
P.39	Davies 6x9cm, Schneider 150mm f 5.6, polarizer
P.40	Davies 6x9cm, Schneider 150mm f 5.6, polarizer
P.41	Davies 6x9cm, Schneider 65mm f 5.6, polarizer
P.42	Davies 6x9cm, Schneider 65mm f 5.6, polarizer
P.43	Davies 6x9cm, Schneider 65mm f 5.6, polarizer
P.44(L)	Davies 6x9cm, Schneider 150mm f 5.6, polarizer
P.44(R)	Davies 6x9cm, Schneider 65mm f 5.6
P.45(L)	Davies 6x9cm, Schneider 150mm f 5.6, polarizer
P.45(R)	Davies 6x9cm, Schneider 65mm f 5.6
P.46	Plaubel 69W, Schneider 47mm f 5.6, polarizer
P.47	Davies 6x9cm, Schneider 65mm f 5.6, polarizer
P.48-52	Konica FS-1, Hexanon 135mm f 4, 2 x Metz 30B flash
P.53(L)	Canon EOS RT, Canon 80-200 f 2.8L zoom, 430 EZ flash
P.53(R)	Konica FS-1, Hexanon 135mm f 4, 2 x Metz 30B flash
P.54	Davies 6x9cm, Schneider 150mm f 5.6, polarizer
P.55	Davies 6x9cm, Schneider 150mm f 5.6, polarizer
P.56	Davies 6x9cm, Schneider 65mm f 5.6, polarizer
P.57	Davies 6x9cm, Schneider 150mm f 5.6
P.58	Davies 6x9cm, Schneider 65mm f 5.6
P.59	Davies 6x9cm, Schneider 65mm f 5.6
P.60	Davies 6x9cm, Schneider 65mm f 5.6, polarizer
P.61	Davies 6x9cm, Schneider 65mm f 5.6, polarizer
P.64	Davies 6x9cm, Schneider 65mm f 5.6, polarizer
P.65	Davies 6x9cm, Nikkor 360mm f 8 ED, polarizer
P.66	Davies 6x9cm, Nikkor 360mm f 8 ED, polarizer
P.67	Davies 6x9cm, Nikkor 360mm f 8 ED, polarizer
P.68	Davies 6x9cm, Nikkor 360mm f 8 ED, polarizer
P.69	Davies 6x9cm, Nikkor 360mm f 8 ED, polarizer
P.70	Davies 6x9cm, Schneider 65mm f 5.6, polarizer
P.71	Rollei 6006, Distagon 40mm f 4
P.72	Rollei 6006, Rolleigon 50mm f 4
P.73	Davies 6x9cm, Schneider 65mm f 5.6
P.74	Canon EOS RT, Canon 20-35mm f 2.8L zoom
P.75	Rollei 6006, Rolleigon 50mm f 4, polarizer
P.76	Davies 6x9cm, Nikkor 360mm f 8 ED, polarizer
P.77	Rollei 6006, Distagon 40mm f 4
P.78	Davies 6x9cm, Nikkor 360mm f 8 ED
P.79	Davies 6x9cm, Schneider 150mm f 5.6, polarizer
P.80	Davies 6x9cm, Nikkor 360mm f 8 ED, polarizer
P.81	Davies 6x9cm, Schneider 150mm f 5.6, polarizer
P.82	Davies 6x9cm, Nikkor 360mm f 8 ED, polarizer
P.83	Rollei 6006, Distagon 40mm f 4
P.84	Davies 6x9cm, Nikkor 360mm f 8 ED
P.85	Davies 6x9cm, Nikkor 360mm f 8 ED
P.88	Rollei 6006, Rolleigon 50mm f 4, polarizer
P.89	Rollei 6006, Rolleigon 50mm f 4, polarizer
P.90	Rollei 6006, Rolleigon 50mm f 4, polarizer
P.91	Rollei 6006, Rolleigon 50mm f 4, polarizer
P.92	Rollei 6006, Planar 80mm f 2.8, polarizer
P.93	Rollei 6006, Planar 80mm f 2.8, polarizer
P.94	Nikon F3, Nikkor 16mm f 2.8 fisheye
P.95	Nikonos III, Nikonos 15mm f 2.8, Ikelite 150 strobe
P.96	Nikon F3, Nikkor 16m f 2.8 fisheye, Ikelite 150 strobe
P.97	Nikonos III, Nikonos 15mm f 2.8, Ikelite 150 strobe
P.98	Nikon F3, Nikkor 60mm f 2.8 micro, Ikelite 150 strobe
P.99	Nikon F3, Nikkor 105mm f 2.8 micro, Ikelite 150 strobe
P.100	Nikon F3, Nikkor 60mm f 2.8 micro, Ikelite 150 strobe
P.101	Nikon F3, Nikkor 60mm f 2.8 micro, Ikelite 150 strobe
P.102	Horseman FA 4x5, Schneider 90mm f 8, polarizer
P.103	Davies 6x9cm, Schneider 65mm f 5.6
P.104	Davies 6x9cm, Nikkor 360mm f 8 ED
P.105	Canon EOS RT, Canon 300mm f 4L, Canon 2x extender
P.106	Davies 6x9cm, Schneider 65mm f 5.6
P.107	Canon EOS RT, Canon 300mm f 4L, Canon 2x extender
P.108	Davies 6x9cm, Schneider 65mm f 5.6, polarizer
P.109	Davies 6x9cm, Schneider 150mm f 5.6
P.110	Davies 6x9cm, Schneider 65mm f 5.6
P.111	Davies 6x9cm, Schneider 65mm f 5.6, polarizer
P.112	Davies 6x9cm, Schneider 150mm f 5.6, polarizer
P.113	Davies 6x9cm, Schneider 65mm f 5.6, polarizer
P.114	Horseman FA 4x5, Schneider 90mm f 8, polarizer
P.115	Davies 6x9cm, Schneider 150mm f 5.6, polarizer
P.116	Canon EOS RT, Canon 300mm f 4L, Canon 2x extender
P.117	Canon EOS RT, Canon 300mm f 4L

Lens equivalents to 35mm format:

20mm	:	Schneider 47mm f 5.6
24mm	:	Distagon 40mm f 4
28mm	:	Schneider 65mm f 5.6 (on 6x9)
		Schneider 90mm f 8 (on 4x5)
		Rolleigon 50mm f 4
50mm	:	Schneider 150mm f 5.6 (on 4x5)
65mm	:	Schneider 150mm f 5.6 (on 6x9)
115mm	:	Nikkor 360mm f 8 ED (on 4x5)
135mm	:	Nikkor 360mm f 8 ED (on 6x9)
Film	:	Fujichrome Velvia and Provia

THE TOP END OF DOWN UNDER
Jarver's first and best selling book looks at
the beauty and diversity of the Top End and
unusual views of Darwin. A feature is the
exciting chapter on the thunderstorms and
lightning of this unique area.
Hardcover 120 pages 250 x 260mm

DARWIN, AUSTRALIA'S NORTHERN CAPITAL
The national parks and unusual flora and fauna
have always intrigued visitors to the Top End.
Along with the natural features, this book looks at
the lifestyle and architecture of Australia's most
multicultural city.
Softcover 60 pages 215 x 286mm

THE HEART OF AUSTRALIA
A stunning series of Uluru (Ayers Rock) in
the rain is a highlight of this book. It takes
you on a tour around the gorges of the
Macdonnell Ranges, the Simpson Desert
and the wildflowers of Central Australia.
Hardcover 120 pages 250 x 260mm

CAIRNS, REEF TO RAINFOREST
The coral reefs and mountainous rainforest
have made Far North Queensland the premier
tourist destination of Northern Australia.
Take a tour through the towns, Tableland
and natural features of our Northern Tropics.
Softcover 64 pages 215 x 286mm

KAKADU COUNTRY
A selection of superb landscapes from
the major national parks of the Top End
including Kakadu. Complementing this,
a further chapter on the majestic skyscapes
of Northern Australia.
Hardcover 120 pages 250 x 260mm

PETER JARVER LANDSCAPE CALENDAR
Australia's spectacular northern landscapes
presented in a functional, large format calendar
by Australia's foremost landscape photographer.
Quality images are also suitable for framing.
Spiral Bound 14 pages 285 x 335mm

Further information on the above calendar and books may be obtained by writing to:

Thunderhead Publishing,
P.O. Box 549 Kuranda, Qld 4872 Australia

First published by Thunderhead Publishing 1996
PO Box 549, Kuranda Qld. 4872 Australia
Telephone (070) 937 171
Facsimile (070) 938 897

Photography by Peter Jarver, Master of Photography, AIPP
Text written by Rod Ritchie
Additional photography by Nick Tonks, Mike Prociv, Mike Trenerry
Concept and photographic layout by Peter Jarver
Design by Two Dogs Barking, Cairns
Separations and film by Graphic Skills, Brisbane
Printed by South China Press, Hong Kong
© Peter Jarver
Daintree to the Coral Sea
ISBN O 9589067 5 0

ACKNOWLEDGEMENTS:
Nick Tonks
for photographs on pages 94 to 101
Mick Prociv
for photographs on pages 48, 49, 50, 51(r), 52, 53(r)
Mike Trenerry
for photograph on page 51(l)
Marilyn Venus for editing assistance
Department of Environment and Heritage
Undara Lava Lodge
Trezise Bush Guides
[1] Ellis Rowan, "A Flower Hunter in Queensland and New Zealand"
1898 - Angus & Robertson

THUNDERHEAD PUBLISHING